Stations of the Scale

A Photographic Memoir About Food and Suffering

Andrea Rosenthal

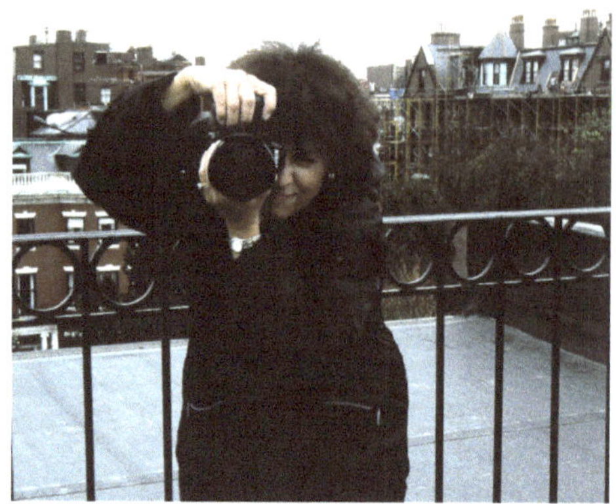

ISBN 978-0-578-02404-2

First edition May 2009
Manufactured in the United States of America

Published by Rosenpho.
Contact rosenpho@comcast.net
www.andrearosenthal.net

Rosenthal, Andrea.
Stations of the scale: a photographic memoir about food and suffering

1. Weight loss. 2. Nutrition. 3. Food habits.
4. Body image.

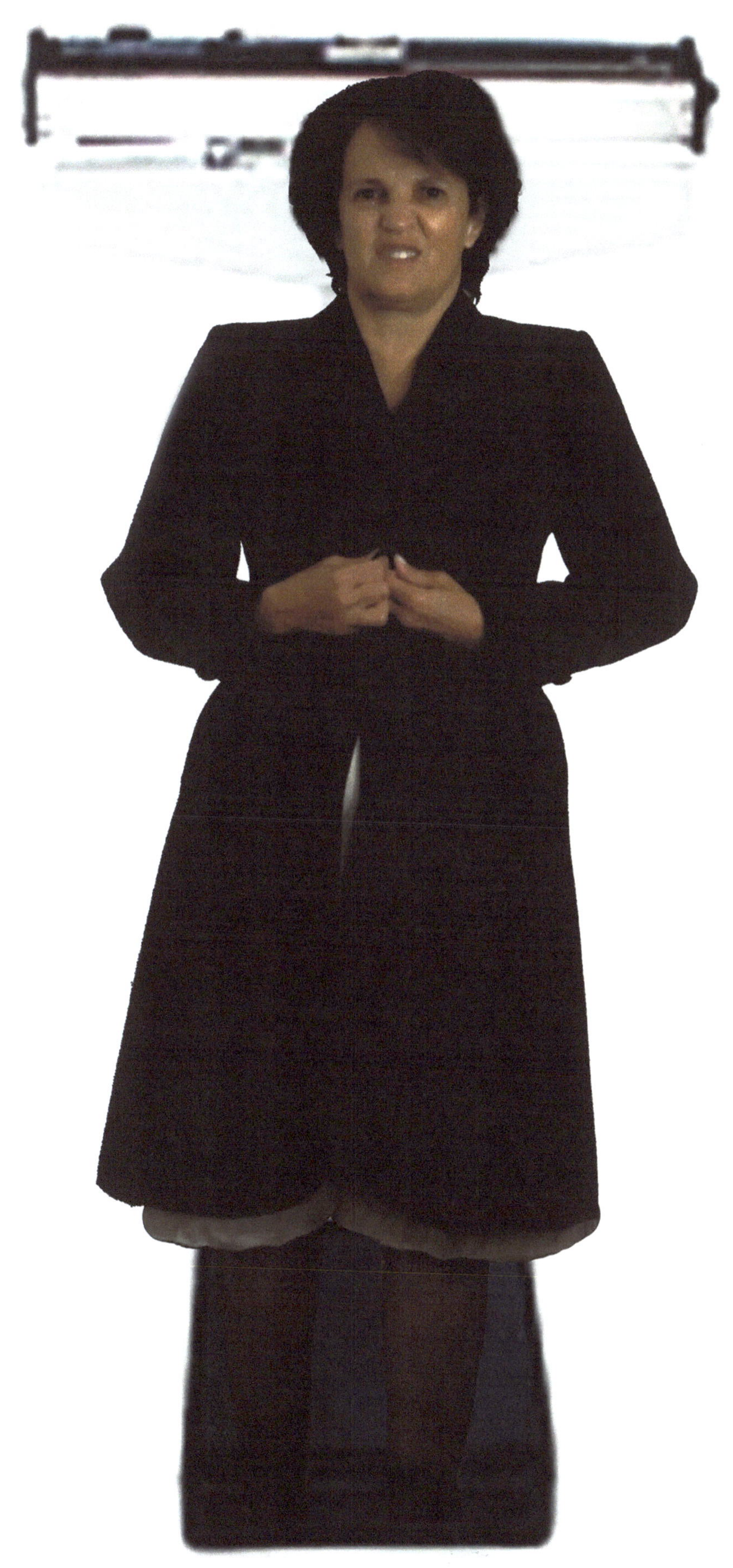

My grandparents' philosophy was Chubby = Healthy + Happy. Understandably so, since fear of famine was real where they came from. One of my grandfathers decided to emigrate from Eastern Europe when all the food he had was 24 beans.

Having enough food was always very important in my family.

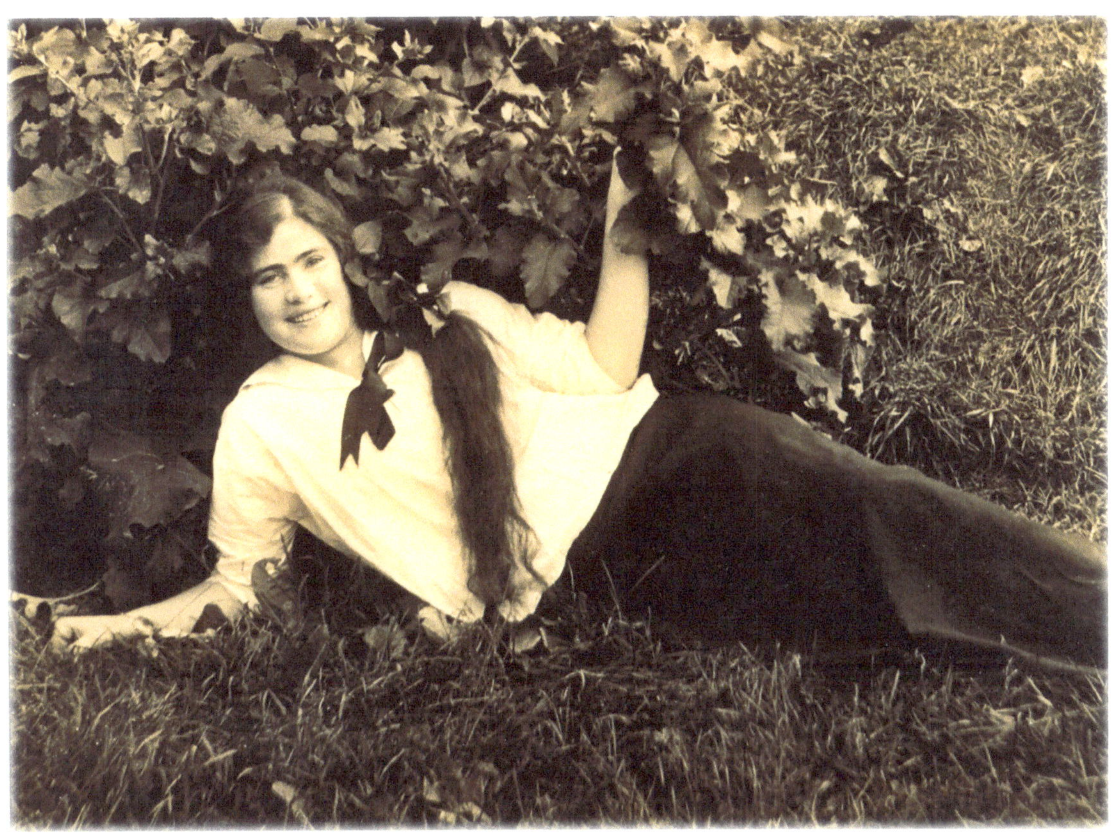

My Grandma Minnie when she was on vacation in the Catskills. She was so well-fed and healthy-looking that the farmer where she boarded would take her in his wagon to meet incoming trains as an advertisement for his place.

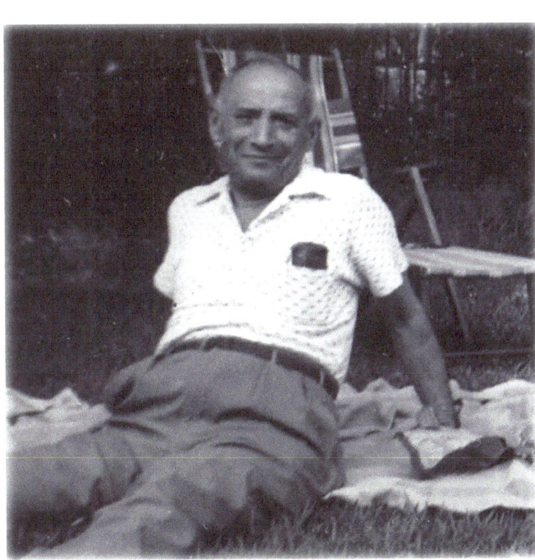

Grandpa Nathan came from Romania, where he learned to like spicy, rich food.

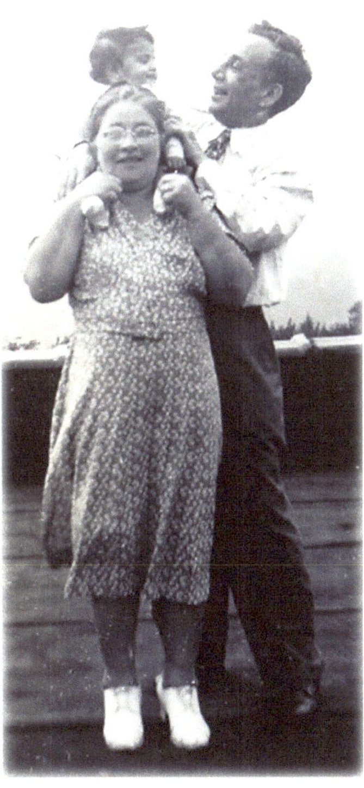

Grandma Rose and Grandpa Gershon, he of the 24 beans.

“Ess, ess, mein kind.” (Yiddish for “Eat, eat, my child.”) The devoted efforts of my parents and grandparents have managed to plump me up from a scrawny 5-pound infant to the 2-year-old chubbette seen here.

I remember this day well. Waiting for the photographer, my mother gave me two slices of cheese, one for each hand. I ate one and thought, “I still have another one,” but looked for it in vain.

Realization dawned -- I had eaten it. The feeling of a disconnect about the relationship of food to reality has stayed with me to this day.

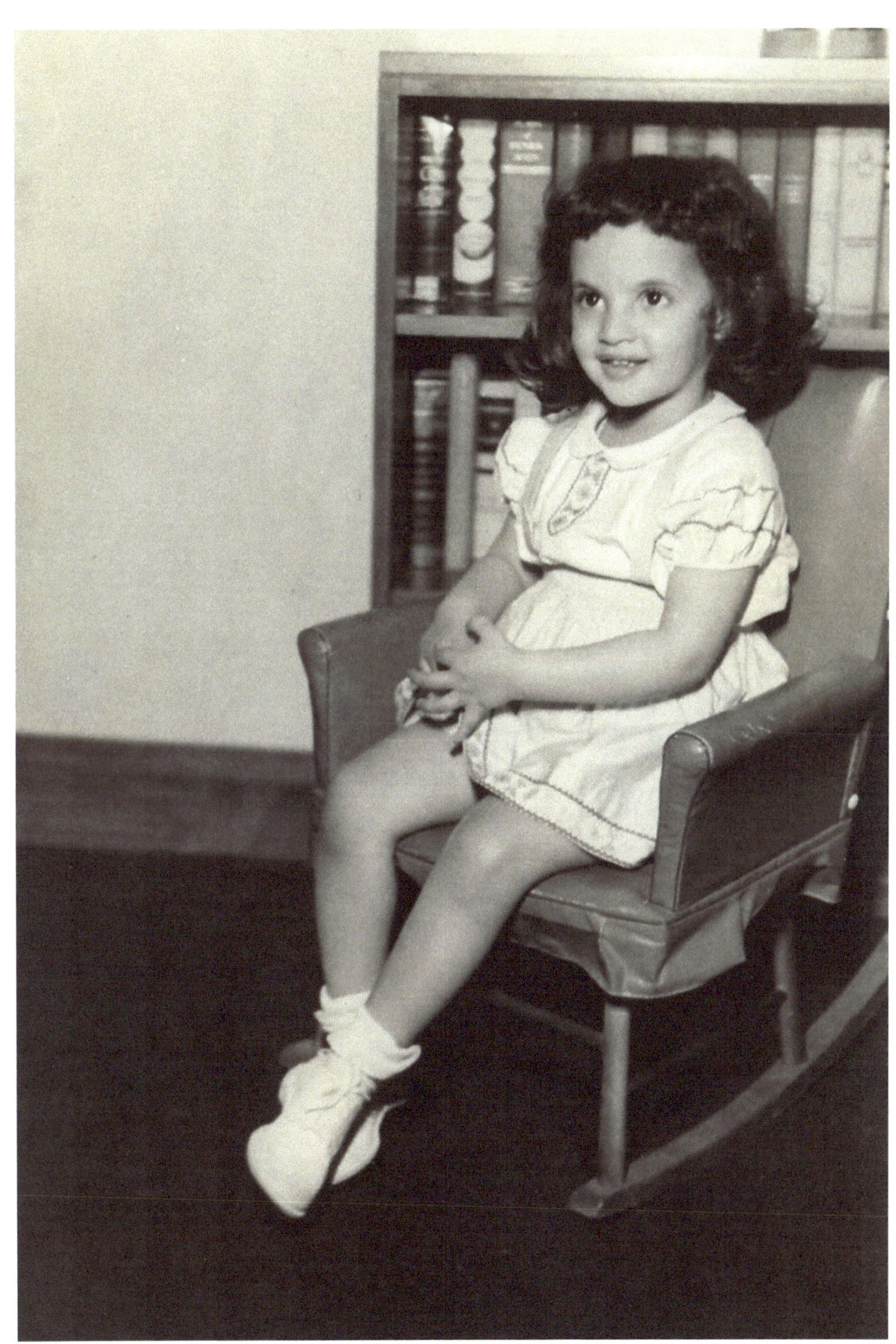

At our house, the dinner table resembled a boxing ring, with a family member in each corner. My sister and father were the usual combatants, fighting about how little she ate.

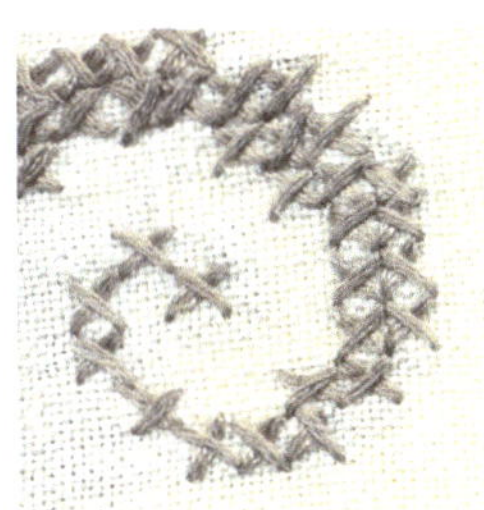

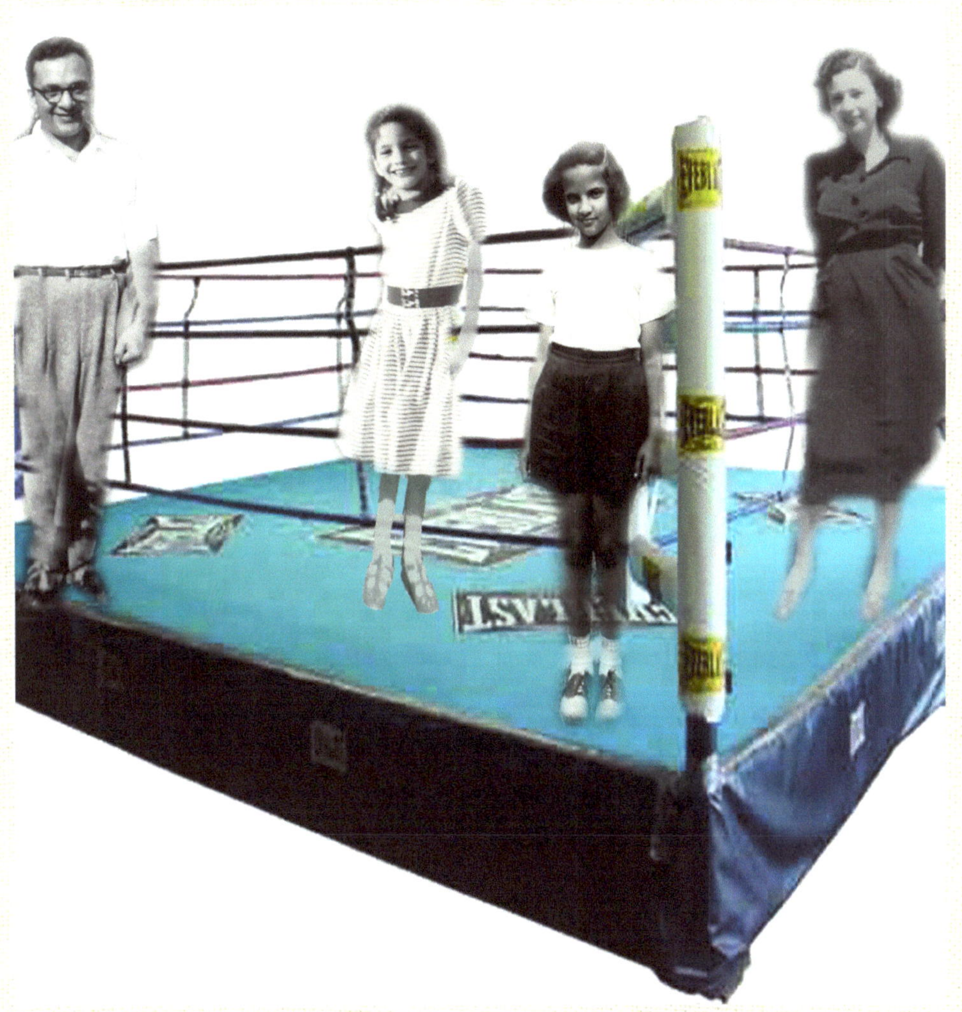

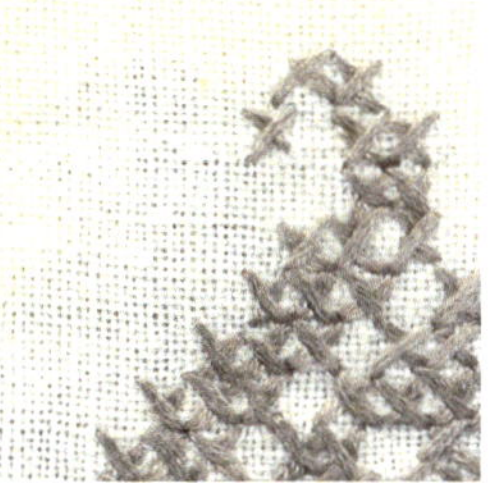

At age twelve, I am 5’2” tall and weigh 124 pounds. The pediatrician tells my mother I am fat and prescribes a diet, sending me into a lifetime of secret eating.

I like anything that starts with “c,” such as cheese, candy, or cookies, preferably eaten while reading. The lies I’ve told myself are common to all addicts, like “I’ll just have one more and then stop.”

This has nothing to do with actual hunger; many times I binged past the point of feeling sick, then went on to eat a full dinner because I didn’t want anyone else to know.

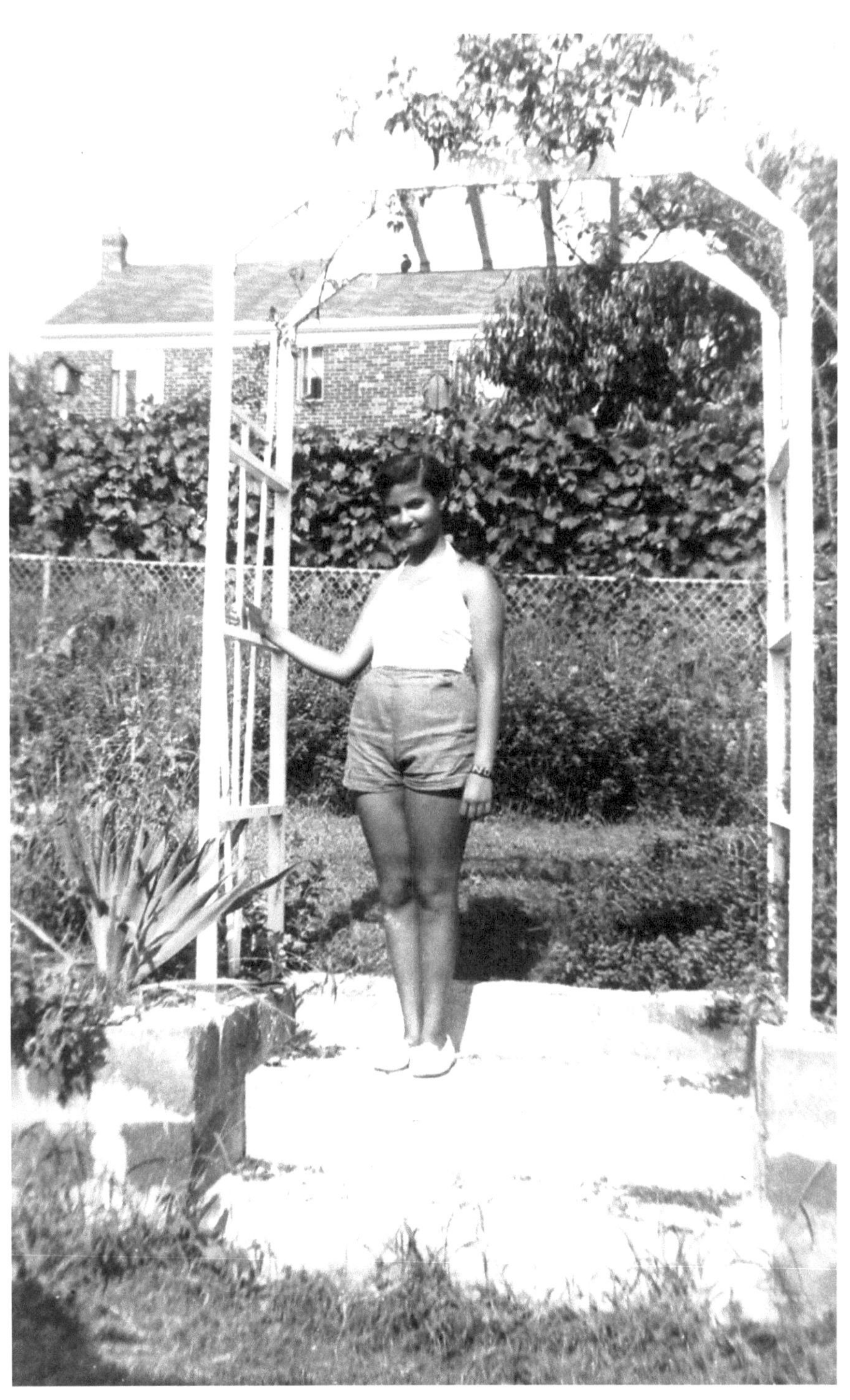

I love reading.

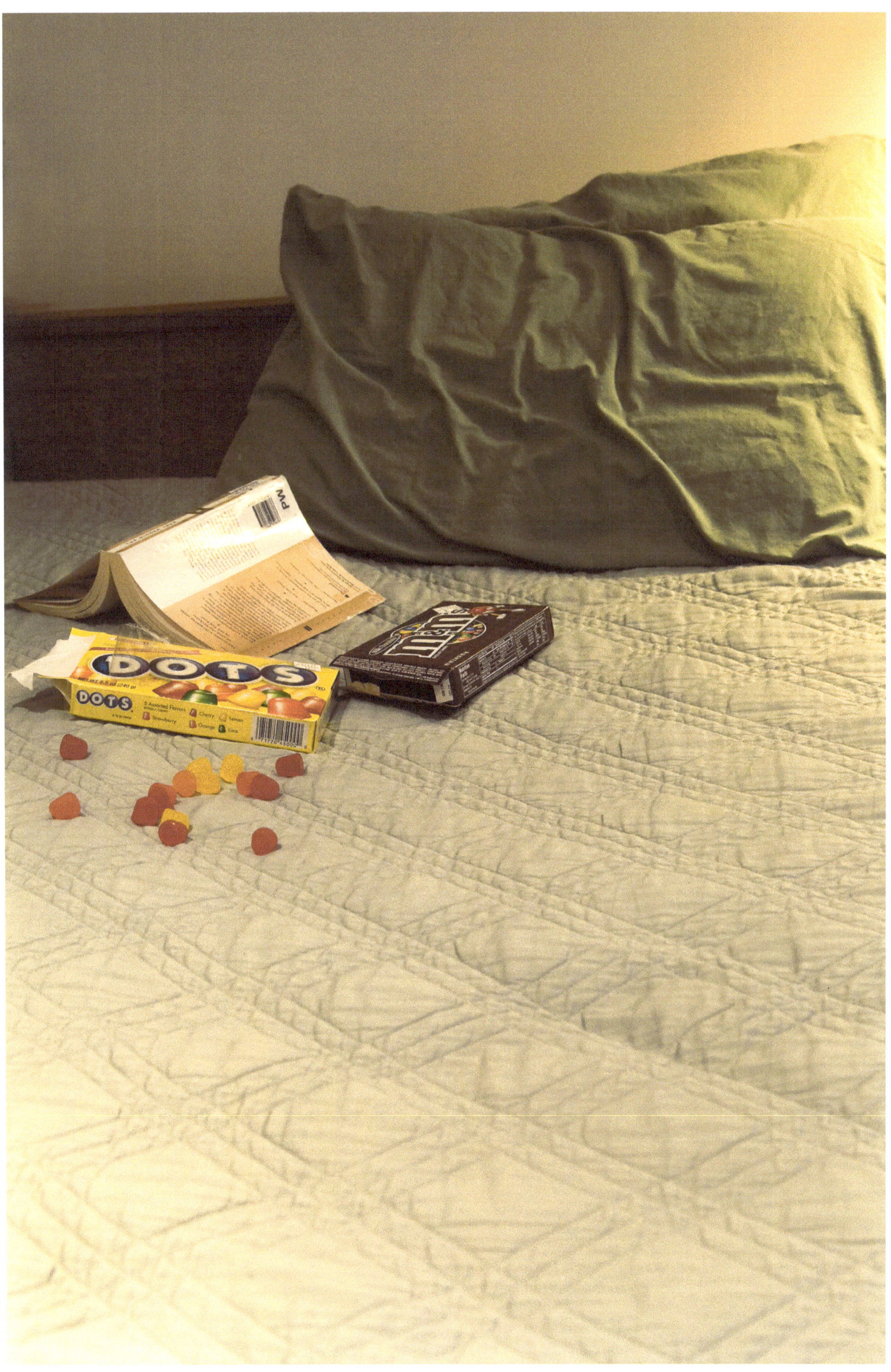
DOTS
DOTS

I know this is the right way to diet, but the problem is, nothing tastes as good as chocolate or anything else sweet.

No matter how big the package might be, the nutrition label should read, “One serving equals entire bag.”

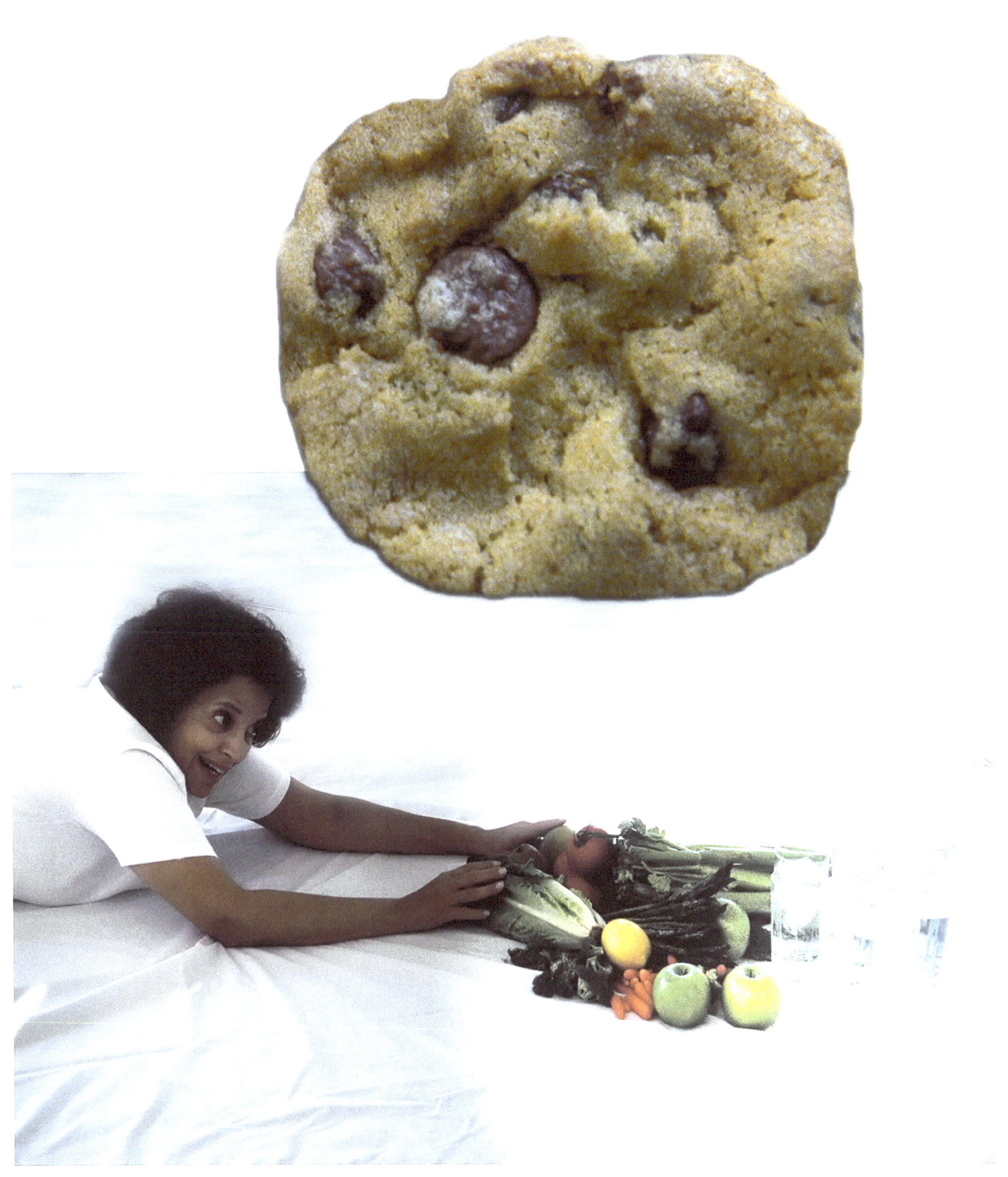

I’m only buying these for trick-or-treaters.

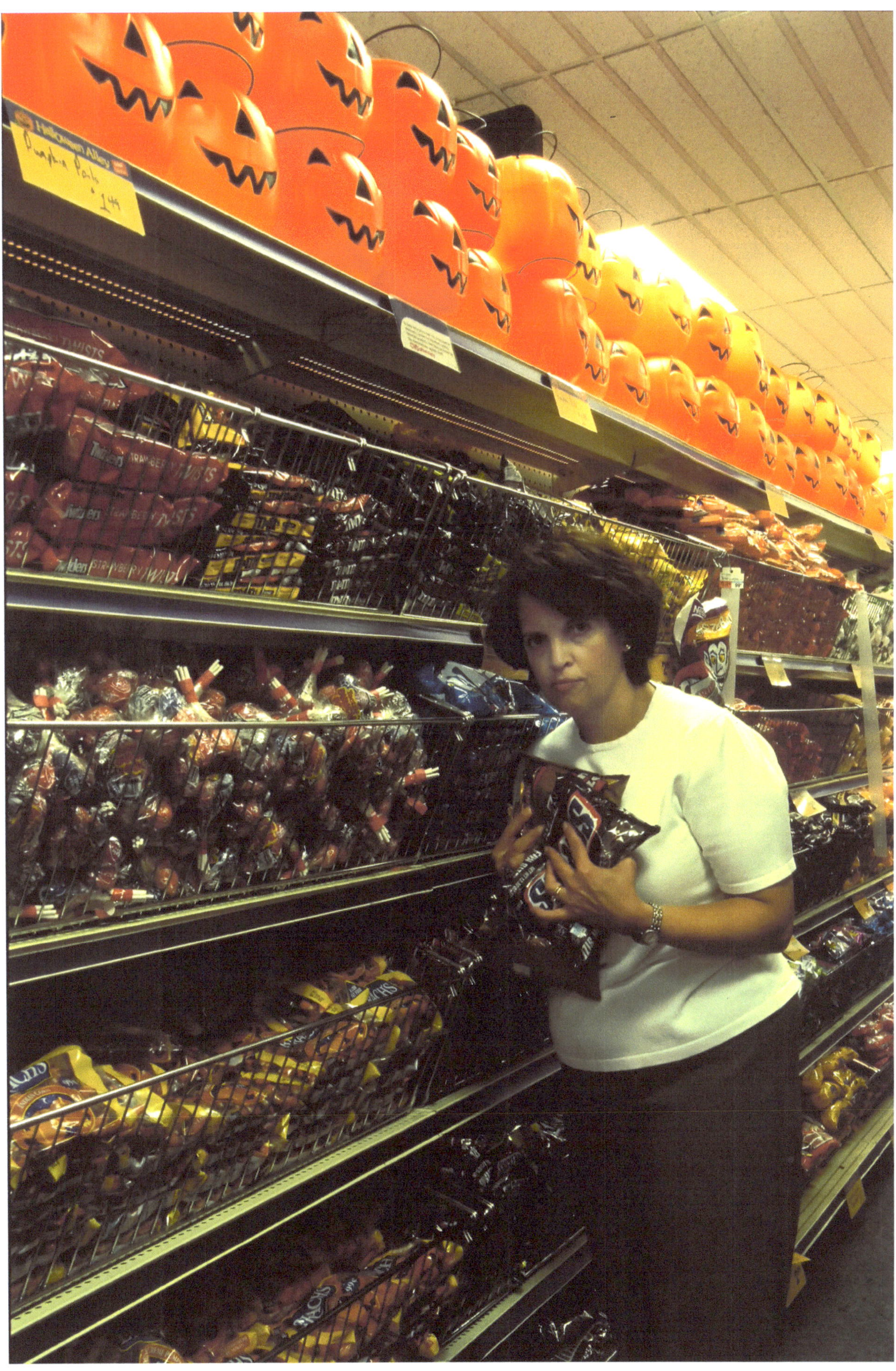
Halloween Alley
Pumpkin Pails
1.44
Twizzlers STRAWBERRY TWISTS

The Scream, or, Enough Already

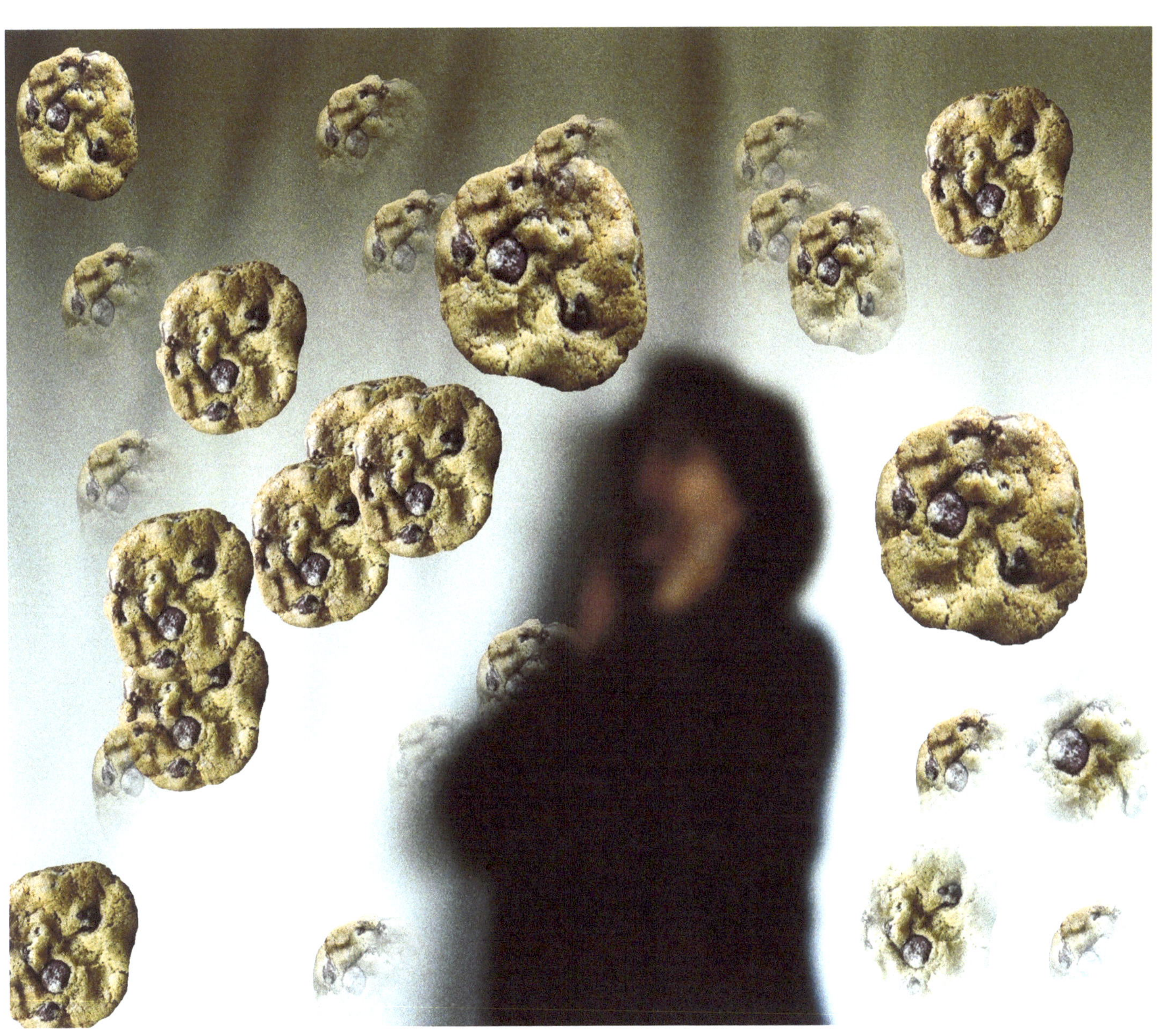

“Maybe I should just apply it directly to my hips.”

(Valerie Harper said these immortal words as Rhoda Morgenstern on “The Mary Tyler Moore Show.”)

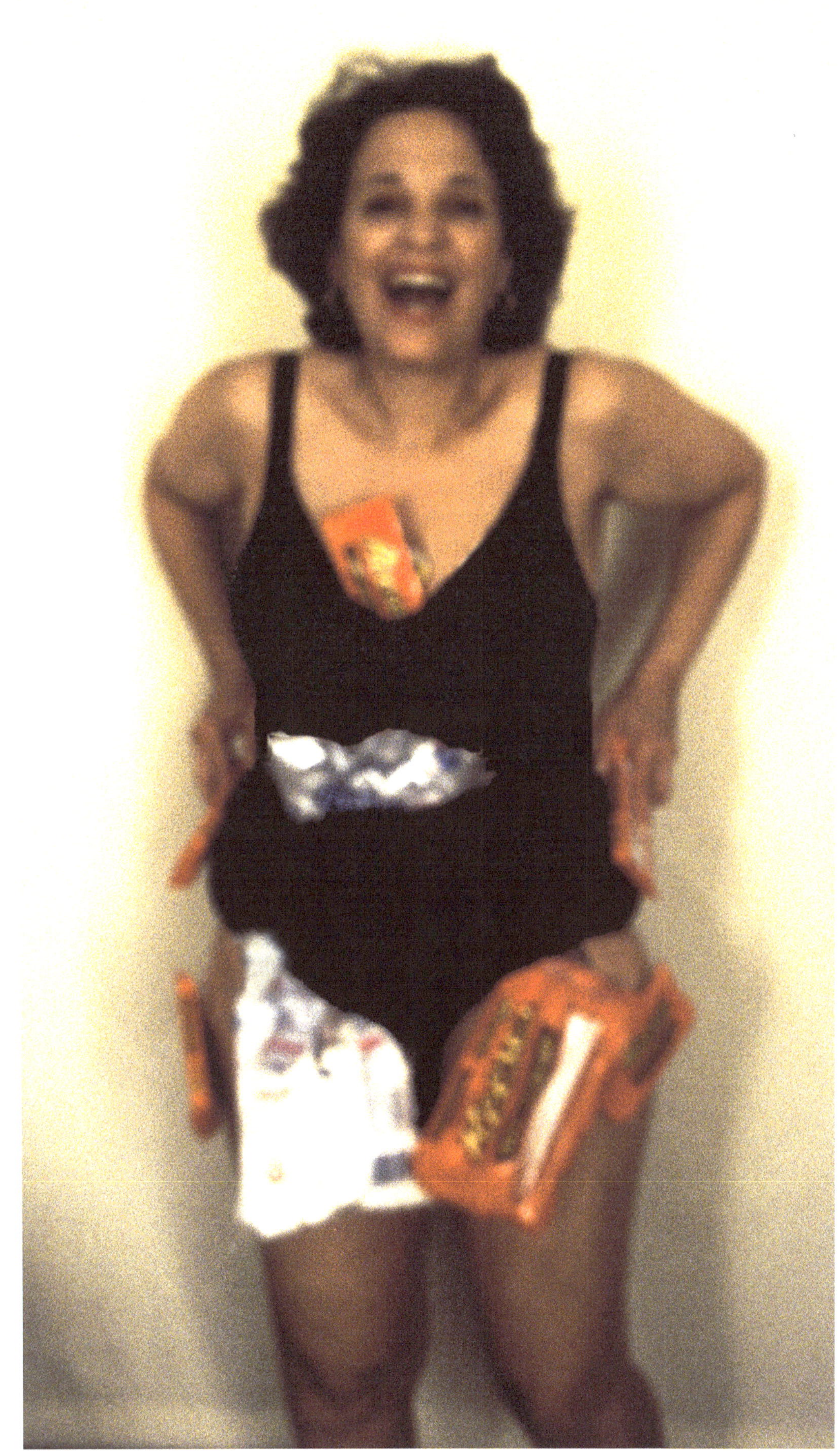

Temptation calls and I give in.
Is candy such an awful sin?

Cookies are not criminals,
They’re balm for all life’s little ills.

How I hope my little sweeties
Will not give me diabetes.

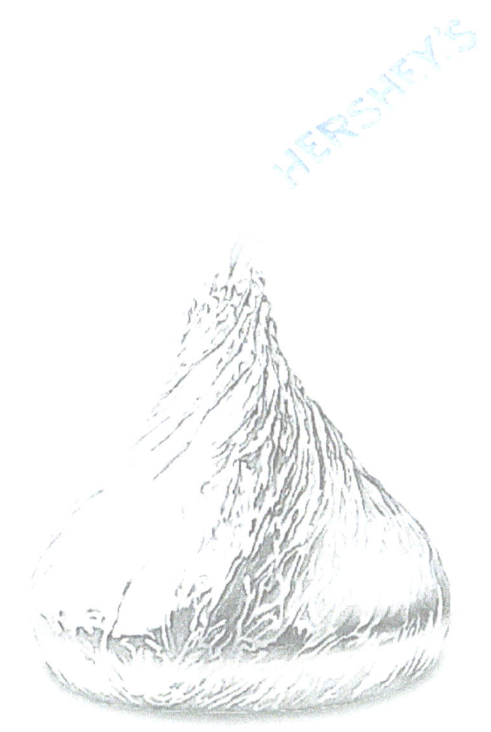
HERSHEY'S

Gain 40 pounds with each child, twice

Move to Greenwich. Gain 5.

Build house at Cape. Gain 5.

Move to Brook Road. Gain 5.

Los
pow

START
wedding

Scale: 1 inch = 5 pounds

Lose 40 pounds both times. Thanks, Diet Workshop.

My life has been a game of Reverse Chutes and Ladders.
I want to get past the ups and downs and end the game.

REVERSE CHUTES AND LADDERS

Move to Boston. Gain 5.

Gain 20 pounds WHILE RUN-NING! (I thought I could eat whatever I wanted.)

Move to condo -- gain 5.

Lose 10 -- Fen-Phen.

Gain 7 back.

Lose 15 with Weight Watchers.

Lose 2 -- for better or worse, I'm accepting myself, decriminalizing cookies, and maintaining.

15 by will
alone.

THE END
(I hope)

At four, unlike my playmate on the right, I must have been asking myself, “This is fun?” which was pretty much how I felt at that time about physical activity.

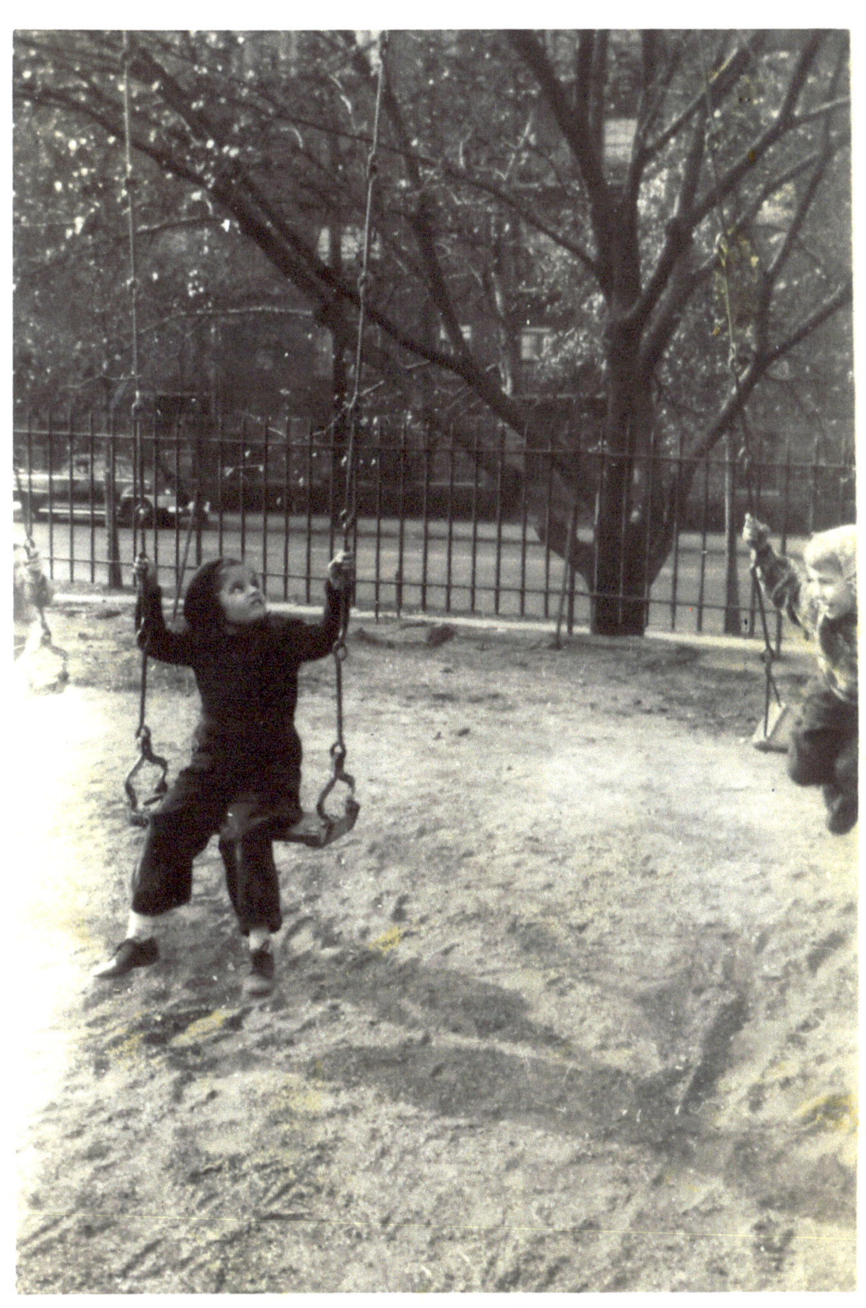

At forty, I took up sports and finally had a good body image.

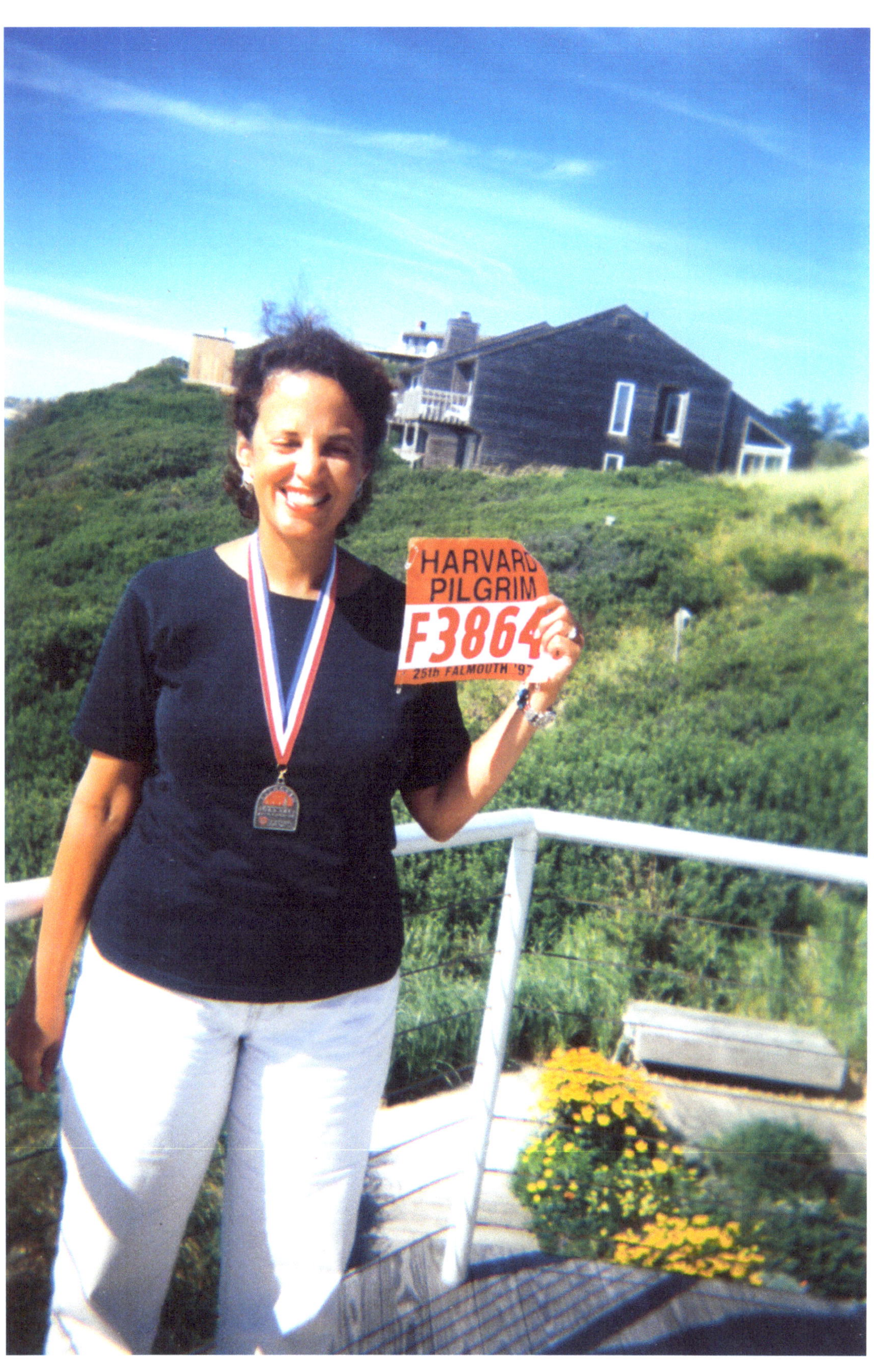
HARVARD
PILGRIM
F3864
25th FALMOUTH '97

Do these stripes make me look fat?

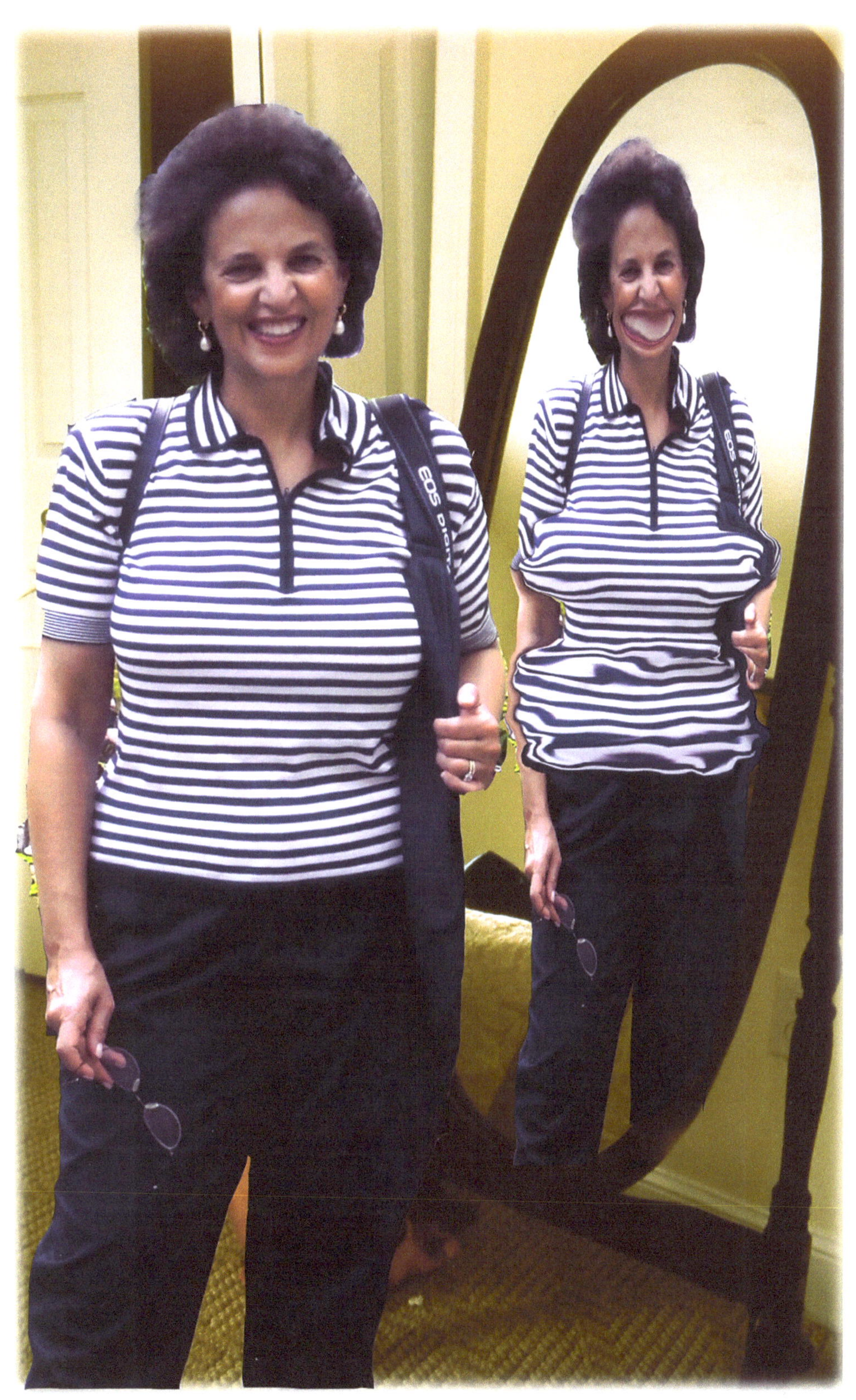
EOS

I’ll wear these again after I lose weight.

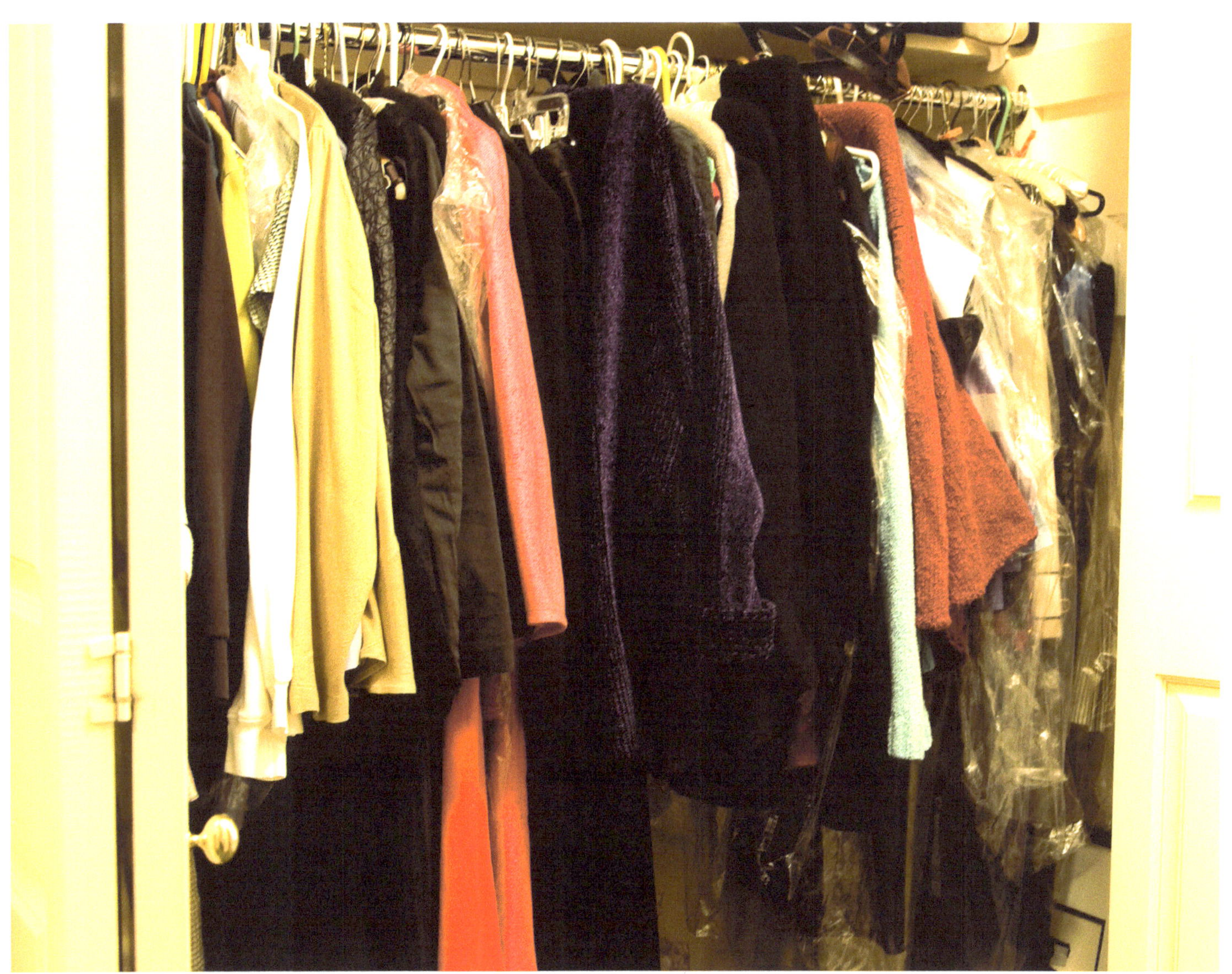

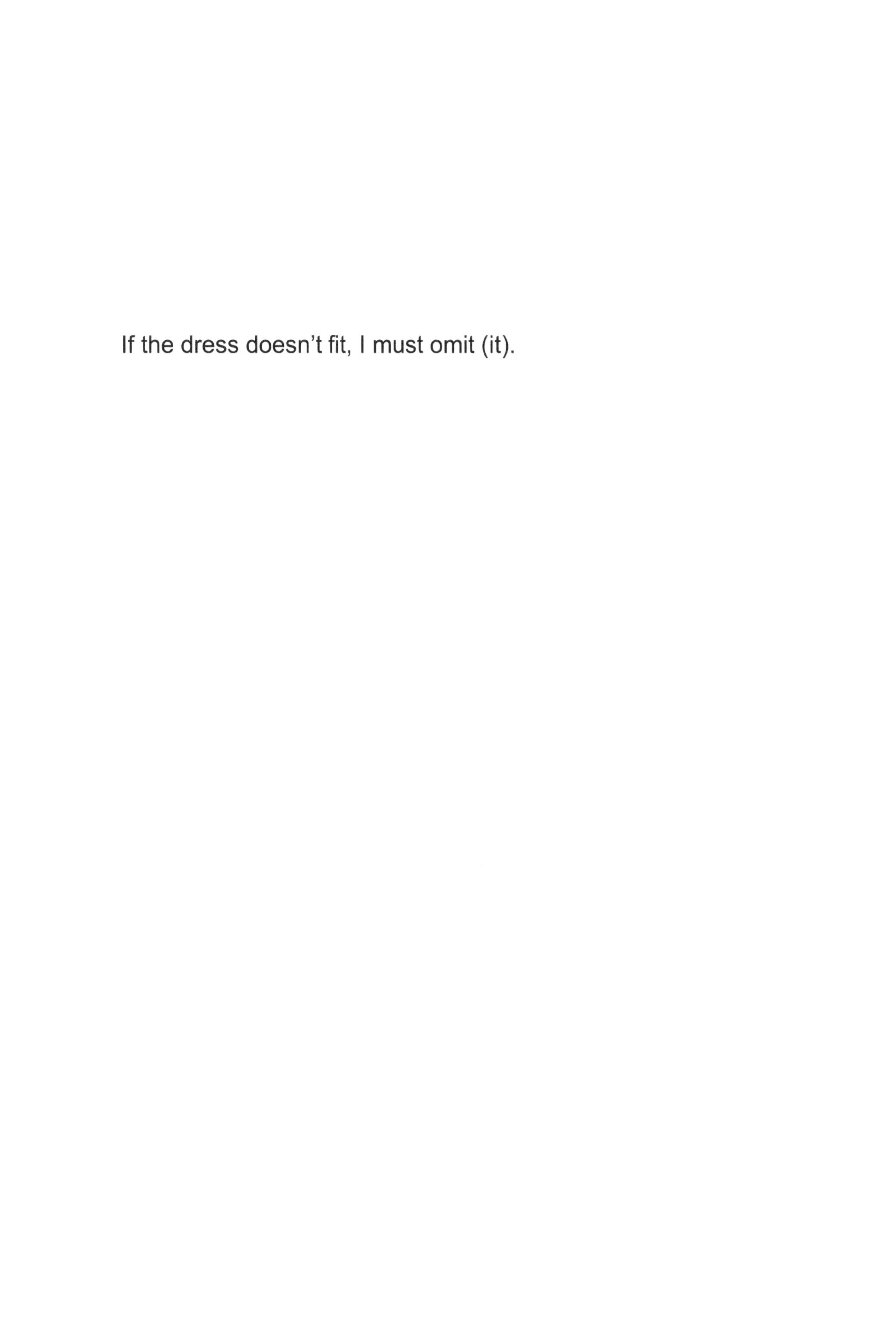

If the dress doesn't fit, I must omit (it).

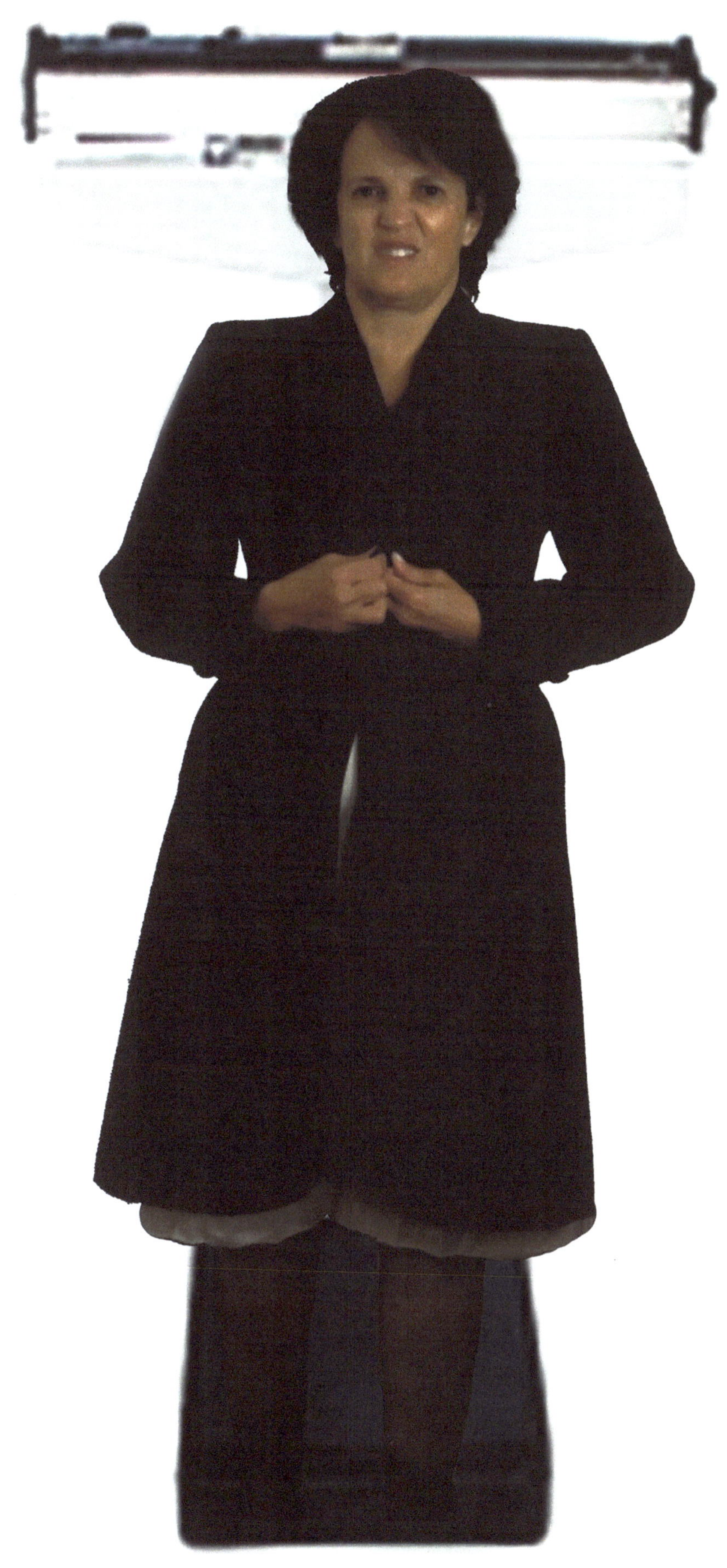

R.I.P.

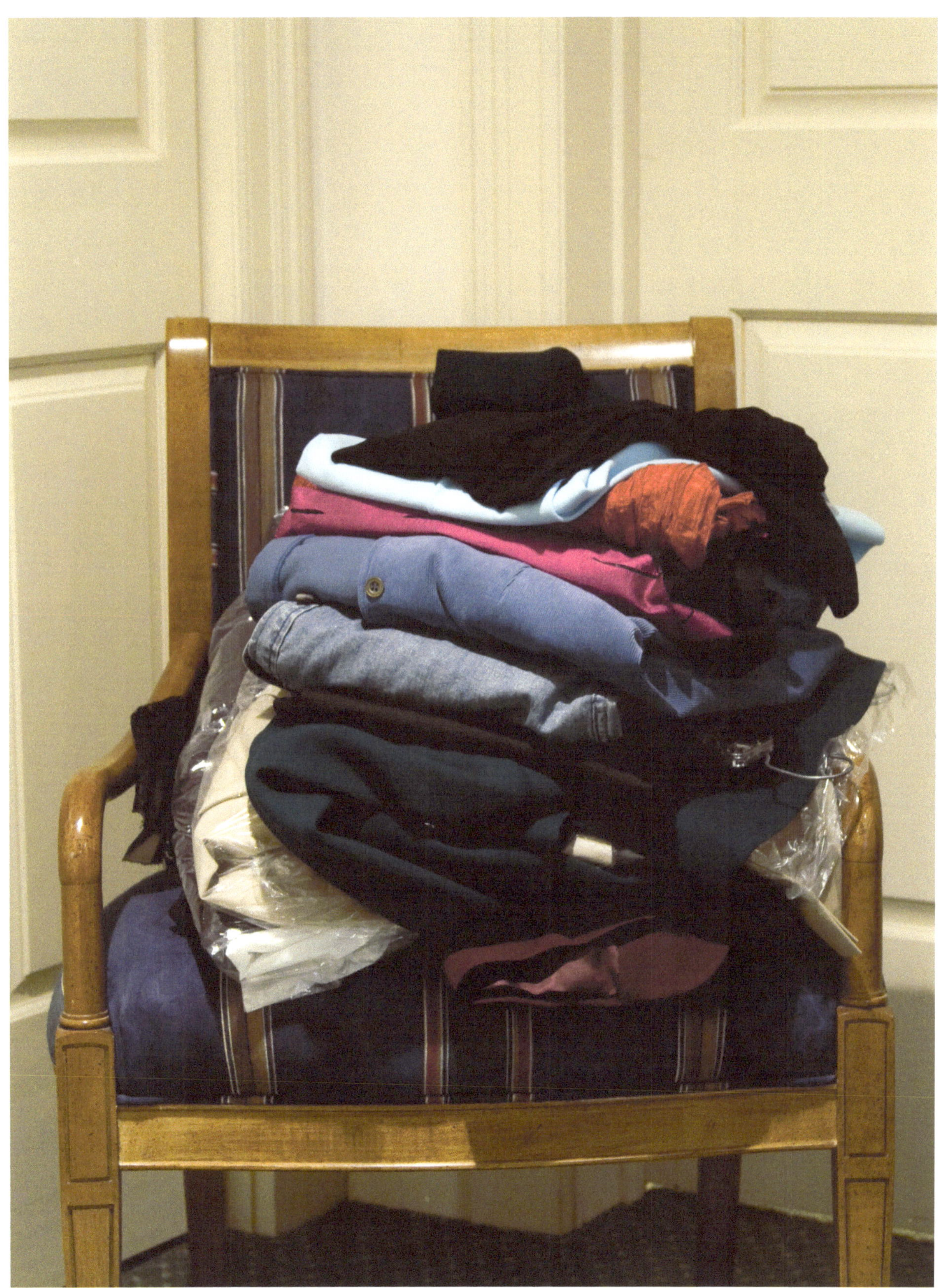

Now I only have clothes that fit
without cruel underwear.

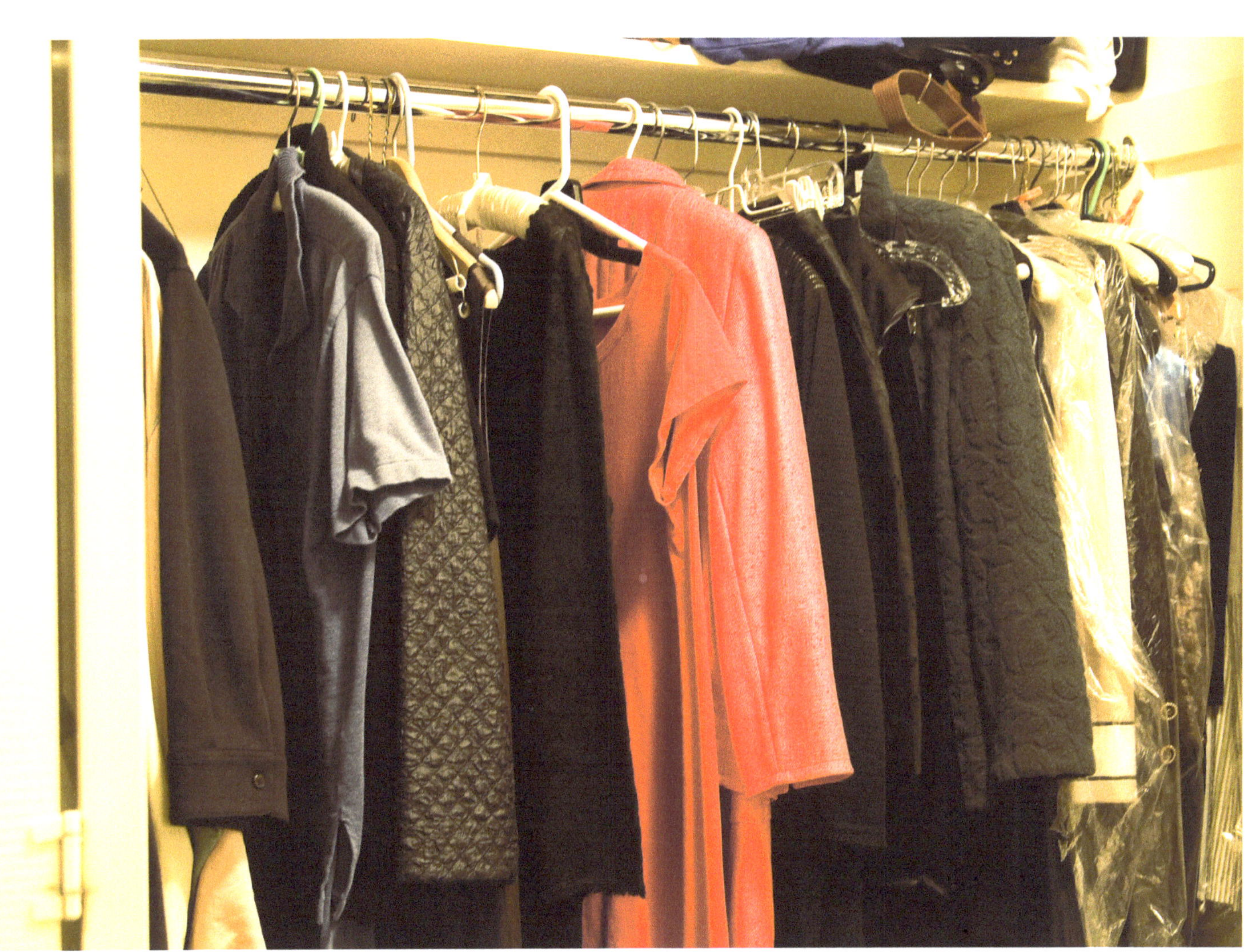

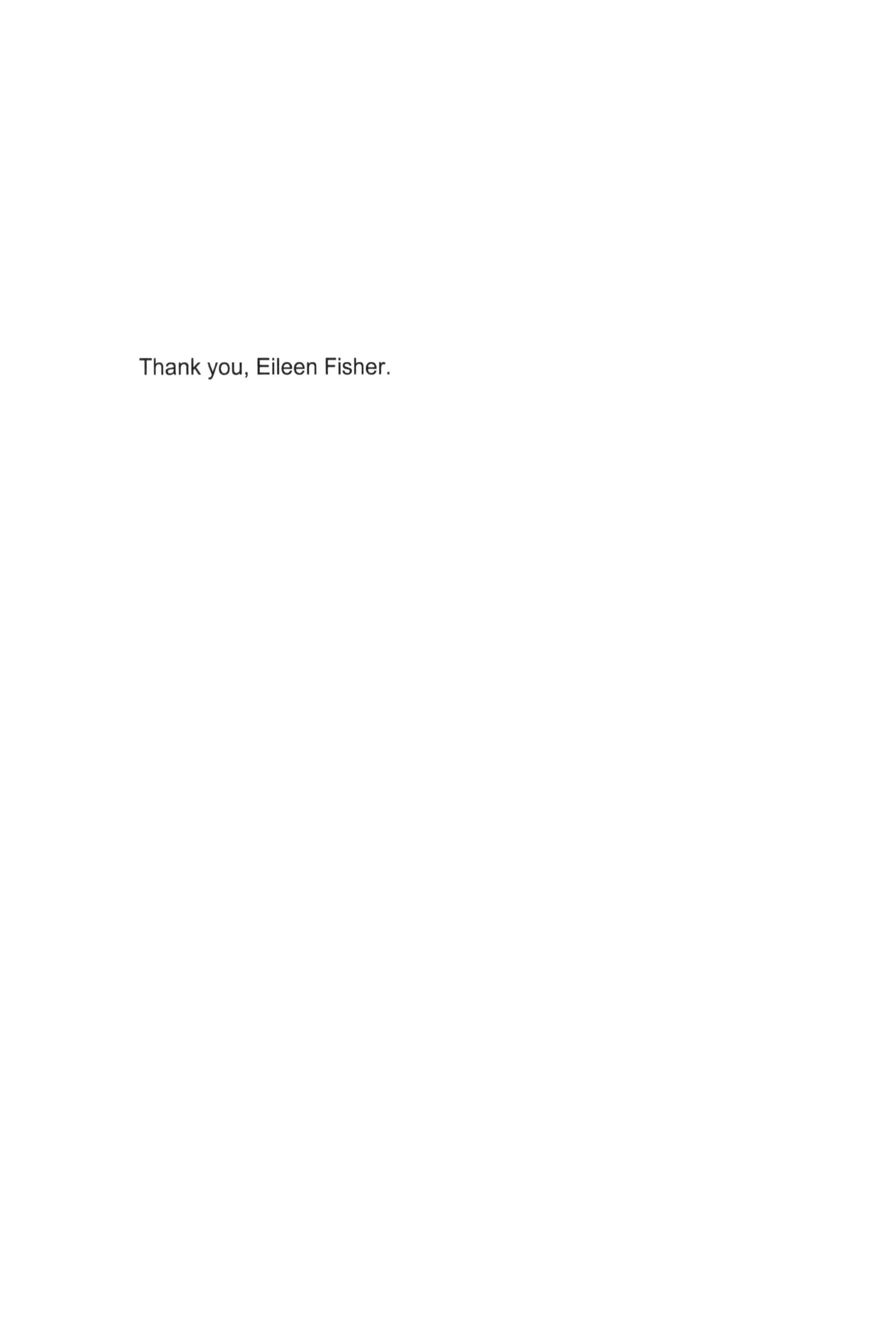

Thank you, Eileen Fisher.

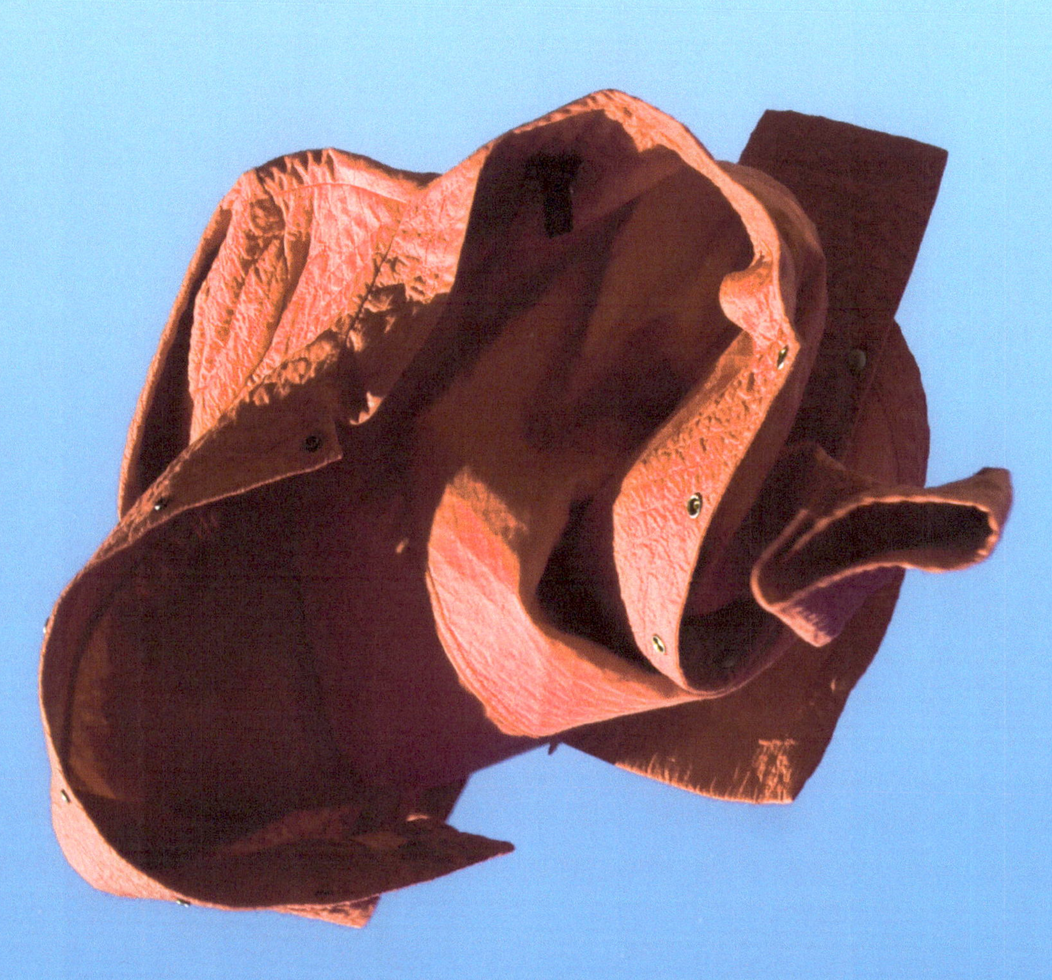

Ta da --
free at last.

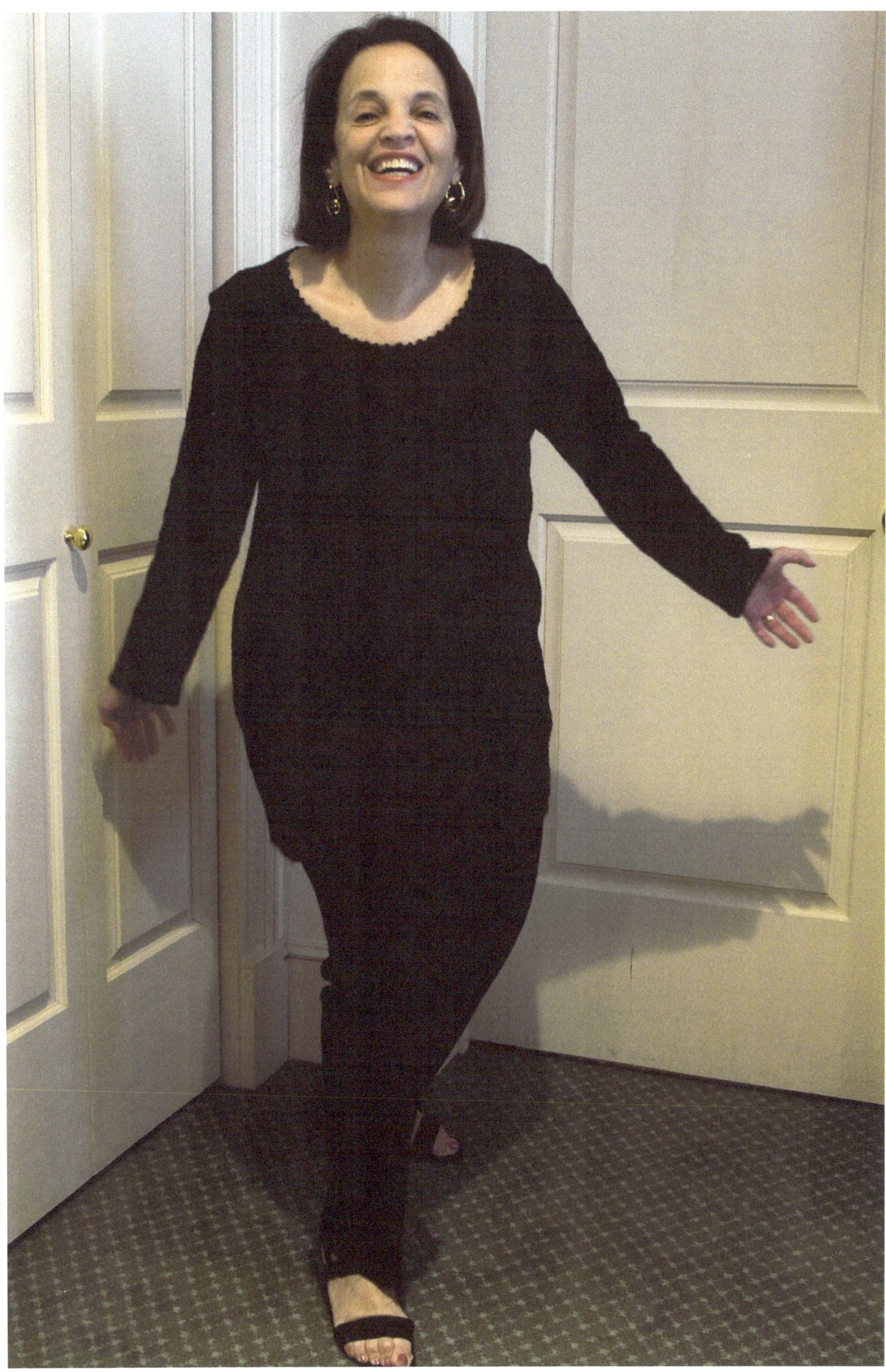

No jellybeans were harmed in
the making of this book.

Well, maybe a few.

FULL DISCLOSURE

The cookies in “The Scream” are all Photoshopped variations of the same cookie.

Originally I baked a big batch of chocolate chip cookies but, before I could photograph them, I ate all except one and had to create the image with the lone survivor.

I would like to thank my husband, Harvey -- without whom.

And our offspring, Sophie, Sally, and Rob, for the inspiring goodness of their lives.

And Joan Leibovich, Karen Davis, and Sharon Miller -- for editing, advice, and tireless assistance.

www.ingramcontent.com/pod-product-compliance
Lightning Source LLC
LaVergne TN
LVHW070154110826
845147LV00002B/398

* 9 7 8 0 5 7 8 0 2 4 0 4 2 *